Daily Planner

_____

By : Adil Daisy

© Copyright 2021

All rights reserved. No parte of this book may be used or reproduced in any manner whatsoever without the prior written permission of the author.

Daily Planner

M T W T F S S

Date _____

MUST DO TODAY:
- ☐
- ☐
- ☐

SCHEDULE + TO-DOS

APPOINTMENTS

TODAY I'M GRATEFUL FOR:

NOTES:

Hydration

Fitness

Meal Plan

Daily Planner

M T W T F S S

Date _____

MUST DO TODAY:
- ☐ _____
- ☐ _____
- ☐ _____

SCHEDULE + TO-DOS
_____
_____
_____
_____
_____
_____
_____
_____
_____
_____
_____
_____
_____
_____
_____
_____

APPOINTMENTS
_____
_____
_____
_____

TODAY I'M GRATEFUL FOR:

NOTES:

Meal Plan

Hydration

Fitness

Daily Planner

M T W T F S S

Date _____

MUST DO TODAY:
-
-
-

SCHEDULE + TO-DOS

APPOINTMENTS

TODAY I'M GRATEFUL FOR:

NOTES:

Hydration

Fitness

Meal Plan

Daily Planner

M T W T F S S

Date _____

MUST DO TODAY:
- ○
- ○
- ○

SCHEDULE + TO-DOS

APPOINTMENTS
_____
_____
_____
_____

TODAY I'M GRATEFUL FOR:

NOTES:

Hydration

Fitness

Meal Plan

Daily Planner

M T W T F S S

Date _____

MUST DO TODAY:
- ☐
- ☐
- ☐

SCHEDULE + TO-DOS

APPOINTMENTS

TODAY I'M GRATEFUL FOR:

NOTES:

Hydration

Fitness

Meal Plan

Daily Planner

M T W T F S S

Date _____

MUST DO TODAY:
- ○ _____
- ○ _____
- ○ _____

SCHEDULE + TO-DOS

_____
_____
_____
_____
_____
_____
_____
_____
_____
_____
_____
_____
_____
_____
_____
_____
_____
_____

Hydration

Fitness

Appointments

_____
_____
_____
_____

TODAY I'M GRATEFUL FOR:

NOTES:

Meal Plan

Daily Planner

M T W T F S S

Date _____

MUST DO TODAY:
- ☐
- ☐
- ☐

SCHEDULE + TO-DOS

APPOINTMENTS

TODAY I'M GRATEFUL FOR:

NOTES:

Hydration

Fitness

Meal Plan

Daily Planner

M T W T F S S

Date _____

MUST DO TODAY:
- ☐ _____
- ☐ _____
- ☐ _____

SCHEDULE + TO-DOS
_____
_____
_____
_____
_____
_____
_____
_____
_____
_____
_____
_____
_____
_____
_____
_____

Appointments
_____
_____
_____
_____

TODAY I'M GRATEFUL FOR:

NOTES:

Hydration

Fitness

Meal Plan

Daily Planner

M T W T F S S

Date _____

MUST DO TODAY:
- _____
- _____
- _____

SCHEDULE + TO-DOS

APPOINTMENTS

TODAY I'M GRATEFUL FOR:

NOTES:

Hydration

Fitness

Meal Plan

Daily Planner

M T W T F S S

Date _____

MUST DO TODAY:
- ○ _____
- ○ _____
- ○ _____

SCHEDULE + TO-DOS

APPOINTMENTS
_____
_____
_____
_____

TODAY I'M GRATEFUL FOR:

NOTES:

Hydration

Fitness

Meal Plan

Daily Planner

M T W T F S S

Date _____

MUST DO TODAY:
-
-
-

SCHEDULE + TO-DOS

APPOINTMENTS

TODAY I'M GRATEFUL FOR:

NOTES:

Hydration

Fitness

Meal Plan

Daily Planner

M T W T F S S

Date _____

MUST DO TODAY:
- ○
- ○
- ○

SCHEDULE + TO-DOS

APPOINTMENTS

TODAY I'M GRATEFUL FOR:

NOTES:

Hydration

Fitness

Meal Plan

Daily Planner

M T W T F S S

Date _____

MUST DO TODAY:
- ○ _____
- ○ _____
- ○ _____

SCHEDULE + TO-DOS

_____
_____
_____
_____
_____
_____
_____
_____
_____
_____
_____
_____
_____

APPOINTMENTS

_____
_____
_____
_____

TODAY I'M GRATEFUL FOR:

NOTES:

Hydration

Fitness

Meal Plan

Daily Planner

M T W T F S S

Date _____

MUST DO TODAY:
- ○
- ○
- ○

SCHEDULE + TO-DOS

Appointments

TODAY I'M GRATEFUL FOR:

NOTES:

Hydration

Fitness

Meal Plan

Daily Planner

M T W T F S S

Date _____

MUST DO TODAY:
- ○
- ○
- ○

SCHEDULE + TO-DOS

APPOINTMENTS

TODAY I'M GRATEFUL FOR:

NOTES:

Hydration

Fitness

Meal Plan

Daily Planner

M T W T F S S

Date _____

MUST DO TODAY:
- ○ _____
- ○ _____
- ○ _____

SCHEDULE + TO-DOS

APPOINTMENTS

TODAY I'M GRATEFUL FOR:

NOTES:

Hydration

Fitness

Meal Plan

Daily Planner

M T W T F S S

Date _____

MUST DO TODAY:
- ○
- ○
- ○

SCHEDULE + TO-DOS

APPOINTMENTS

TODAY I'M GRATEFUL FOR:

NOTES:

Hydration

Fitness

Meal Plan

Daily Planner

M T W T F S S

Date _____

MUST DO TODAY:
- ○
- ○
- ○

SCHEDULE + TO-DOS

APPOINTMENTS

TODAY I'M GRATEFUL FOR:

NOTES:

Hydration

Fitness

Meal Plan

Daily Planner

M T W T F S S

Date _____

MUST DO TODAY:
-
-
-

SCHEDULE + TO-DOS

APPOINTMENTS

TODAY I'M GRATEFUL FOR:

NOTES:

Hydration

Fitness

Meal Plan

Daily Planner

M T W T F S S

Date _____

MUST DO TODAY:
- ○
- ○
- ○

SCHEDULE + TO-DOS

APPOINTMENTS

TODAY I'M GRATEFUL FOR:

NOTES:

Hydration

Fitness

Meal Plan

Daily Planner

M T W T F S S

Date _____

MUST DO TODAY:
- ○
- ○
- ○

SCHEDULE + TO-DOS

APPOINTMENTS

TODAY I'M GRATEFUL FOR:

NOTES:

Hydration

Fitness

Meal Plan

Daily Planner

M T W T F S S

Date _____

MUST DO TODAY:
- ○
- ○
- ○

SCHEDULE + TO-DOS

APPOINTMENTS

TODAY I'M GRATEFUL FOR:

NOTES:

Hydration

Fitness

Meal Plan

Daily Planner

M T W T F SS

Date _____

MUST DO TODAY:
- ☐ _____
- ☐ _____
- ☐ _____

SCHEDULE + TO-DOS

APPOINTMENTS

TODAY I'M GRATEFUL FOR:

NOTES:

Hydration

Fitness

Meal Plan

Daily Planner

M T W T F S S

Date _____

MUST DO TODAY:
- ○
- ○
- ○

SCHEDULE + TO-DOS

APPOINTMENTS

TODAY I'M GRATEFUL FOR:

NOTES:

Hydration

Fitness

Meal Plan

Daily Planner

M T W T F S S

Date _____

MUST DO TODAY:
- ○
- ○
- ○

SCHEDULE + TO-DOS

APPOINTMENTS

TODAY I'M GRATEFUL FOR:

NOTES:

Hydration

Fitness

Meal Plan

Daily Planner

M T W T F S S

Date _____

MUST DO TODAY:
-
-
-

SCHEDULE + TO-DOS
_____
_____
_____
_____
_____
_____
_____
_____
_____
_____
_____
_____
_____
_____
_____
_____

APPOINTMENTS
_____
_____
_____
_____

TODAY I'M GRATEFUL FOR:

NOTES:

Hydration

Fitness

Meal Plan

Daily Planner

M T W T F S S

Date _____

MUST DO TODAY:
- ○
- ○
- ○

SCHEDULE + TO-DOS

APPOINTMENTS

TODAY I'M GRATEFUL FOR:

NOTES:

Hydration

Fitness

Meal Plan

Daily Planner

M T W T F S S

Date _____

MUST DO TODAY:
- ○
- ○
- ○

SCHEDULE + TO-DOS

APPOINTMENTS
_____
_____
_____
_____
_____

TODAY I'M GRATEFUL FOR:

NOTES:

Hydration

Fitness

Meal Plan

Daily Planner

M T W T F S S

Date _____

MUST DO TODAY:
-
-
-

SCHEDULE + TO-DOS

APPOINTMENTS

TODAY I'M GRATEFUL FOR:

NOTES:

Hydration

Fitness

Meal Plan

Daily Planner

M T W T F S S

Date _____

MUST DO TODAY:
- _____
- _____
- _____

SCHEDULE + TO-DOS

_____
_____
_____
_____
_____
_____
_____
_____
_____
_____
_____
_____
_____
_____
_____

APPOINTMENTS
_____
_____
_____
_____
_____

TODAY I'M GRATEFUL FOR:

NOTES:

Hydration

Fitness

Meal Plan

Daily Planner

M T W T F S S

Date _____

MUST DO TODAY:
-
-
-

SCHEDULE + TO-DOS

APPOINTMENTS

TODAY I'M GRATEFUL FOR:

NOTES:

Hydration

Fitness

Meal Plan

Daily Planner

M T W T F S S

Date _____

MUST DO TODAY:
- ○ _____
- ○ _____
- ○ _____

SCHEDULE + TO-DOS

_____
_____
_____
_____
_____
_____
_____
_____
_____
_____
_____
_____
_____
_____

APPOINTMENTS

_____
_____
_____
_____
_____

TODAY I'M GRATEFUL FOR:

NOTES:

Hydration

Fitness

Meal Plan

Daily Planner

M T W T F S S

Date _____

MUST DO TODAY:
- ○ _____
- ○ _____
- ○ _____

SCHEDULE + TO-DOS

APPOINTMENTS

TODAY I'M GRATEFUL FOR:

NOTES:

Hydration

Fitness

Meal Plan

Daily Planner

M T W T F S S

Date _____

MUST DO TODAY:
- ○ _____
- ○ _____
- ○ _____

SCHEDULE + TO-DOS

APPOINTMENTS
_____
_____
_____
_____
_____

TODAY I'M GRATEFUL FOR:

NOTES:

Hydration

Fitness

Meal Plan

Daily Planner

M T W T F S S

Date _____

MUST DO TODAY:
- _____
- _____
- _____

SCHEDULE + TO-DOS

APPOINTMENTS

TODAY I'M GRATEFUL FOR:

NOTES:

Hydration

Fitness

Meal Plan

Daily Planner

M T W T F S S

Date _____

MUST DO TODAY:
-
-
-

SCHEDULE + TO-DOS

APPOINTMENTS

TODAY I'M GRATEFUL FOR:

NOTES:

Hydration

Fitness

Meal Plan

Daily Planner

M T W T F S S

Date _____

MUST DO TODAY:
-
-
-

SCHEDULE + TO-DOS

APPOINTMENTS

TODAY I'M GRATEFUL FOR:

NOTES:

Hydration

Fitness

Meal Plan

Daily Planner

M T W T F S S

Date _____

MUST DO TODAY:
- ○ _____
- ○ _____
- ○ _____

SCHEDULE + TO-DOS
_____
_____
_____
_____
_____
_____
_____
_____
_____
_____
_____
_____
_____
_____

APPOINTMENTS
_____
_____
_____
_____

TODAY I'M GRATEFUL FOR:

NOTES:

Hydration

Fitness

Meal Plan

Daily Planner

M T W T F S S

Date _____

MUST DO TODAY:
- _____
- _____
- _____

SCHEDULE + TO-DOS

APPOINTMENTS

TODAY I'M GRATEFUL FOR:

NOTES:

Hydration

Fitness

Meal Plan

Daily Planner

M T W T F S S

Date _____

MUST DO TODAY:
○ _____
○ _____
○ _____

SCHEDULE + TO-DOS

Appointments

_____
_____
_____
_____

TODAY I'M GRATEFUL FOR:

NOTES:

Hydration

Fitness

Meal Plan

Daily Planner

M T W T F S S

Date _____

MUST DO TODAY:
-
-
-

SCHEDULE + TO-DOS

APPOINTMENTS

TODAY I'M GRATEFUL FOR:

NOTES:

Meal Plan

Hydration

Fitness

Daily Planner

M T W T F S S

Date _____

MUST DO TODAY:
- ☐ _____
- ☐ _____
- ☐ _____

SCHEDULE + TO-DOS

APPOINTMENTS

TODAY I'M GRATEFUL FOR:

NOTES:

Hydration

Fitness

Meal Plan

Daily Planner

M T W T F S S

Date _____

MUST DO TODAY:
○
○
○

SCHEDULE + TO-DOS

APPOINTMENTS

TODAY I'M GRATEFUL FOR:

NOTES:

Meal Plan

Hydration

Fitness

Daily Planner

M T W T F S S

Date _____

MUST DO TODAY:
- ○ _____
- ○ _____
- ○ _____

SCHEDULE + TO-DOS

APPOINTMENTS
_____
_____
_____
_____

TODAY I'M GRATEFUL FOR:

NOTES:

Hydration

Fitness

Meal Plan

Daily Planner

M T W T F S S

Date _____

MUST DO TODAY:
- _____
- _____
- _____

SCHEDULE + TO-DOS

APPOINTMENTS

TODAY I'M GRATEFUL FOR:

NOTES:

Hydration

Fitness

Meal Plan

Daily Planner

M T W T F S S

Date _____

MUST DO TODAY:
- ○ _____
- ○ _____
- ○ _____

SCHEDULE + TO-DOS

Appointments

TODAY I'M GRATEFUL FOR:

NOTES:

Hydration

Fitness

Meal Plan

Daily Planner

M T W T F S S

Date _____

MUST DO TODAY:
- _____
- _____
- _____

SCHEDULE + TO-DOS

APPOINTMENTS
_____
_____
_____

TODAY I'M GRATEFUL FOR:

NOTES:

Hydration

Fitness

Meal Plan

Daily Planner

M T W T F S S

Date _____

MUST DO TODAY:
- ☐ _____
- ☐ _____
- ☐ _____

SCHEDULE + TO-DOS

APPOINTMENTS
_____
_____
_____
_____

TODAY I'M GRATEFUL FOR:

NOTES:

Hydration

Fitness

Meal Plan

Daily Planner

M T W T F S S

Date _____

MUST DO TODAY:
- _____
- _____
- _____

SCHEDULE + TO-DOS

APPOINTMENTS

TODAY I'M GRATEFUL FOR:

NOTES:

Hydration

Fitness

Meal Plan

Daily Planner

M T W T F S S

Date _____

MUST DO TODAY:
- ☐ _____
- ☐ _____
- ☐ _____

SCHEDULE + TO-DOS

APPOINTMENTS

TODAY I'M GRATEFUL FOR:

NOTES:

Hydration

Fitness

Meal Plan

Daily Planner

M T W T F S S

Date _____

MUST DO TODAY:
- ○ _____
- ○ _____
- ○ _____

SCHEDULE + TO-DOS

APPOINTMENTS

TODAY I'M GRATEFUL FOR:

NOTES:

Hydration

Fitness

Meal Plan

Daily Planner

M T W T F S S

Date _____

MUST DO TODAY:
-
-
-

SCHEDULE + TO-DOS

APPOINTMENTS

TODAY I'M GRATEFUL FOR:

NOTES:

Hydration

Fitness

Meal Plan

Daily Planner

M T W T F S S

Date _____

MUST DO TODAY:
- ○
- ○
- ○

SCHEDULE + TO-DOS

APPOINTMENTS

TODAY I'M GRATEFUL FOR:

NOTES:

Hydration

Fitness

Meal Plan

Daily Planner

M T W T F S S

Date _____

MUST DO TODAY:
- ○
- ○
- ○

SCHEDULE + TO-DOS

APPOINTMENTS

TODAY I'M GRATEFUL FOR:

NOTES:

Hydration

Fitness

Meal Plan

Daily Planner

M T W T F S S

Date _____

MUST DO TODAY:
-
-
-

SCHEDULE + TO-DOS

APPOINTMENTS

TODAY I'M GRATEFUL FOR:

NOTES:

Hydration

Fitness

Meal Plan

Daily Planner

M T W T F S S

Date _____

MUST DO TODAY:
- ○
- ○
- ○

SCHEDULE + TO-DOS

APPOINTMENTS

TODAY I'M GRATEFUL FOR:

NOTES:

Hydration

Fitness

Meal Plan

Daily Planner

M T W T F S S

Date _____

MUST DO TODAY:
- ○
- ○
- ○

SCHEDULE + TO-DOS

APPOINTMENTS

TODAY I'M GRATEFUL FOR:

NOTES:

Hydration

Fitness

Meal Plan

Daily Planner

M T W T F S S

Date _____

MUST DO TODAY:
-
-
-

SCHEDULE + TO-DOS

APPOINTMENTS

TODAY I'M GRATEFUL FOR:

NOTES:

Hydration

Fitness

Meal Plan

Daily Planner

M T W T F S S

Date _____

MUST DO TODAY:
- ○
- ○
- ○

SCHEDULE + TO-DOS

APPOINTMENTS

TODAY I'M GRATEFUL FOR:

NOTES:

Hydration

Fitness

Meal Plan

Daily Planner

M T W T F S S

Date _____

MUST DO TODAY:
○ _____
○ _____
○ _____

SCHEDULE + TO-DOS
_____
_____
_____
_____
_____
_____
_____
_____
_____
_____
_____
_____
_____
_____
_____
_____

APPOINTMENTS
_____
_____
_____
_____
_____

TODAY I'M GRATEFUL FOR:

NOTES:

Hydration

Fitness

Meal Plan

Daily Planner

M T W T F S S

Date _____

MUST DO TODAY:
- ☐ _____
- ☐ _____
- ☐ _____

SCHEDULE + TO-DOS

_____
_____
_____
_____
_____
_____
_____
_____
_____
_____
_____
_____
_____
_____

APPOINTMENTS

_____
_____
_____

TODAY I'M GRATEFUL FOR:

NOTES:

Hydration

Fitness

Meal Plan

Daily Planner

M T W T F S S

Date _____

MUST DO TODAY:
- ○
- ○
- ○

SCHEDULE + TO-DOS

APPOINTMENTS

TODAY I'M GRATEFUL FOR:

NOTES:

Hydration

Fitness

Meal Plan

Daily Planner

M T W T F S S

Date _____

MUST DO TODAY:
- ◯
- ◯
- ◯

SCHEDULE + TO-DOS

_____
_____
_____
_____
_____
_____
_____
_____
_____
_____
_____
_____
_____
_____
_____
_____

APPOINTMENTS

_____
_____
_____
_____

TODAY I'M GRATEFUL FOR:

NOTES:

Meal Plan

Hydration

Fitness

Daily Planner

M T W T F S S

Date _____

MUST DO TODAY:
- ○
- ○
- ○

SCHEDULE | TO-DOS

APPOINTMENTS

TODAY I'M GRATEFUL FOR:

NOTES:

Hydration

Fitness

Meal Plan

Daily Planner

M T W T F S S

Date _____

MUST DO TODAY:
-
-
-

SCHEDULE + TO-DOS

APPOINTMENTS

TODAY I'M GRATEFUL FOR:

NOTES:

Hydration

Fitness

Meal Plan

Daily Planner

M T W T F S S

Date _____

MUST DO TODAY:
- ○
- ○
- ○

SCHEDULE + TO-DOS

_____
_____
_____
_____
_____
_____
_____
_____
_____
_____
_____
_____
_____
_____
_____
_____

Hydration

Fitness

APPOINTMENTS
_____
_____
_____
_____

TODAY I'M GRATEFUL FOR:

NOTES:

Meal Plan

Daily Planner

M T W T F S S

Date _____

MUST DO TODAY:
- ○ _____
- ○ _____
- ○ _____

SCHEDULE + TO-DOS

APPOINTMENTS

TODAY I'M GRATEFUL FOR:

NOTES:

Hydration

Fitness

Meal Plan

Daily Planner

M T W T F S S

Date _____

MUST DO TODAY:
- ○
- ○
- ○

SCHEDULE + TO-DOS
_____
_____
_____
_____
_____
_____
_____
_____
_____
_____
_____
_____
_____
_____
_____
_____

APPOINTMENTS
_____
_____
_____
_____
_____

TODAY I'M GRATEFUL FOR:

NOTES:

Hydration

Fitness

Meal Plan

Daily Planner

M T W T F S S

Date _____

MUST DO TODAY:
-
-
-

SCHEDULE + TO-DOS

APPOINTMENTS

TODAY I'M GRATEFUL FOR:

NOTES:

Hydration

Fitness

Meal Plan

Daily Planner

M T W T F S S

Date _____

MUST DO TODAY:
- ○
- ○
- ○

SCHEDULE + TO-DOS
_____
_____
_____
_____
_____
_____
_____
_____
_____
_____
_____
_____
_____
_____
_____
_____

Hydration
🥛🥛🥛🥛
🥛🥛🥛🥛

APPOINTMENTS
_____
_____
_____
_____
_____

TODAY I'M GRATEFUL FOR:

NOTES:

Fitness

Meal Plan

Daily Planner

M T W T F S S

Date _____

MUST DO TODAY:
- ☐ _____
- ☐ _____
- ☐ _____

SCHEDULE + TO-DOS

APPOINTMENTS

TODAY I'M GRATEFUL FOR:

NOTES:

Hydration

Fitness

Meal Plan

Daily Planner

M T W T F S S

Date _____

MUST DO TODAY:
- ☐ _____
- ☐ _____
- ☐ _____

SCHEDULE + TO-DOS

Hydration

Appointments

_____
_____
_____
_____
_____

TODAY I'M GRATEFUL FOR:

NOTES:

Fitness

Meal Plan

Daily Planner

M T W T F S S

Date _____

MUST DO TODAY:
- ○
- ○
- ○

SCHEDULE + TO-DOS

APPOINTMENTS

TODAY I'M GRATEFUL FOR:

NOTES:

Hydration

Fitness

Meal Plan

Daily Planner

M T W T F S S

Date _____

MUST DO TODAY:
- ☐ _____
- ☐ _____
- ☐ _____

SCHEDULE + TO-DOS

APPOINTMENTS

TODAY I'M GRATEFUL FOR:

NOTES:

Hydration

Fitness

Meal Plan

Daily Planner

M T W T F S S

Date _____

MUST DO TODAY:
- ○
- ○
- ○

SCHEDULE + TO-DOS

APPOINTMENTS

TODAY I'M GRATEFUL FOR:

NOTES:

Hydration

Fitness

Meal Plan

Daily Planner

M T W T F S S

Date _____

MUST DO TODAY:
○ _____
○ _____
○ _____

SCHEDULE + TO-DOS

APPOINTMENTS

TODAY I'M GRATEFUL FOR:

NOTES:

Hydration

Fitness

Meal Plan

Daily Planner

M T W T F S S

Date _____

MUST DO TODAY:
- ○
- ○
- ○

SCHEDULE + TO-DOS

APPOINTMENTS

TODAY I'M GRATEFUL FOR:

NOTES:

Meal Plan

Hydration

Fitness

Daily Planner

M T W T F S S

Date _____

APPOINTMENTS
_____
_____
_____
_____

MUST DO TODAY:
○ _____
○ _____
○ _____
○ _____

TODAY I'M GRATEFUL FOR:

SCHEDULE + TO-DOS
_____
_____
_____
_____
_____
_____
_____
_____
_____
_____
_____
_____
_____
_____
_____
_____

NOTES:

Hydration

Fitness

Meal Plan

Daily Planner

M T W T F S S

Date _____

MUST DO TODAY:
-
-
-

SCHEDULE + TO-DOS

APPOINTMENTS

TODAY I'M GRATEFUL FOR:

NOTES:

Hydration

Fitness

Meal Plan

Daily Planner

M T W T F S S

Date _____

MUST DO TODAY:
- ○ _____
- ○ _____
- ○ _____

SCHEDULE + TO-DOS

APPOINTMENTS

TODAY I'M GRATEFUL FOR:

NOTES:

Hydration

Fitness

Meal Plan

Daily Planner

M T W T F S S

Date _____

MUST DO TODAY:
- ○ _____
- ○ _____
- ○ _____

SCHEDULE + TO-DOS

APPOINTMENTS

TODAY I'M GRATEFUL FOR:

NOTES:

Hydration

Fitness

Meal Plan

Daily Planner

M T W T F S S

Date _____

MUST DO TODAY:
- ☐ _____
- ☐ _____
- ☐ _____

SCHEDULE + TO-DOS

APPOINTMENTS

TODAY I'M GRATEFUL FOR:

NOTES:

Hydration

Fitness

Meal Plan

Daily Planner

M T W T F S S

Date _____

MUST DO TODAY:
- ○ _____
- ○ _____
- ○ _____

SCHEDULE + TO-DOS

_____
_____
_____
_____
_____
_____
_____
_____
_____
_____
_____
_____
_____
_____

APPOINTMENTS
_____
_____
_____

TODAY I'M GRATEFUL FOR:

NOTES:

Hydration

Fitness

Meal Plan

Daily Planner

M T W T F S S

Date _____

MUST DO TODAY:
○ _____
○ _____
○ _____

SCHEDULE + TO-DOS
_____
_____
_____
_____
_____
_____
_____
_____
_____
_____
_____
_____
_____
_____
_____
_____
_____

APPOINTMENTS
_____
_____
_____
_____

TODAY I'M GRATEFUL FOR:

NOTES:

Hydration

Fitness

Meal Plan

Daily Planner

M T W T F S S

Date _____

MUST DO TODAY:
- ○
- ○
- ○

SCHEDULE + TO-DOS

APPOINTMENTS

TODAY I'M GRATEFUL FOR:

NOTES:

Hydration

Fitness

Meal Plan

Daily Planner

M T W T F S S

Date _____

MUST DO TODAY:
- ○ _____
- ○ _____
- ○ _____

SCHEDULE + TO-DOS

_____
_____
_____
_____
_____
_____
_____
_____
_____
_____
_____
_____
_____
_____
_____
_____
_____
_____

Hydration

Fitness

APPOINTMENTS

_____
_____
_____
_____

TODAY I'M GRATEFUL FOR:

NOTES:

Meal Plan

Daily Planner

M T W T F S S

Date _____

MUST DO TODAY:
- ○
- ○
- ○

SCHEDULE + TO-DOS

_____
_____
_____
_____
_____
_____
_____
_____
_____
_____
_____
_____
_____
_____
_____

APPOINTMENTS

_____
_____
_____
_____

TODAY I'M GRATEFUL FOR:

NOTES:

Hydration

Fitness

Meal Plan

Daily Planner

M T W T F S S

Date _____

MUST DO TODAY:
○ _____
○ _____
○ _____

SCHEDULE + TO-DOS

APPOINTMENTS

TODAY I'M GRATEFUL FOR:

NOTES:

Hydration

Fitness

Meal Plan

Daily Planner

M T W T F S S

Date _____

APPOINTMENTS

MUST DO TODAY:
-
-
-

SCHEDULE + TO-DOS

TODAY I'M GRATEFUL FOR:

NOTES:

Hydration

Fitness

Meal Plan

Daily Planner

M T W T F S S

Date _____

MUST DO TODAY:
- ○ _____
- ○ _____
- ○ _____

SCHEDULE + TO-DOS
_____
_____
_____
_____
_____
_____
_____
_____
_____
_____
_____
_____
_____
_____
_____
_____

APPOINTMENTS
_____
_____
_____
_____
_____

TODAY I'M GRATEFUL FOR:

NOTES:

Hydration

Fitness

Meal Plan

Daily Planner

M T W T F S S

Date _____

MUST DO TODAY:
- ☐ _____
- ☐ _____
- ☐ _____

SCHEDULE + TO-DOS

APPOINTMENTS

TODAY I'M GRATEFUL FOR:

NOTES:

Hydration

Fitness

Meal Plan

Daily Planner

M T W T F S S

Date _____

MUST DO TODAY:
- ○
- ○
- ○

SCHEDULE + TO-DOS

APPOINTMENTS

TODAY I'M GRATEFUL FOR:

NOTES:

Hydration

Fitness

Meal Plan

Daily Planner

M T W T F S S

Date _____

MUST DO TODAY:
- ☐
- ☐
- ☐

SCHEDULE + TO-DOS

APPOINTMENTS

TODAY I'M GRATEFUL FOR:

NOTES:

Hydration

Fitness

Meal Plan

Daily Planner

M T W T F S S

Date _____

MUST DO TODAY:
- ☐ _____
- ☐ _____
- ☐ _____

SCHEDULE + TO-DOS

Appointments

_____
_____
_____
_____

TODAY I'M GRATEFUL FOR:

NOTES:

Hydration

Fitness

Meal Plan

Daily Planner

M T W T F S S

Date _____

MUST DO TODAY:
- ○
- ○
- ○

SCHEDULE + TO-DOS

APPOINTMENTS

TODAY I'M GRATEFUL FOR:

NOTES:

Hydration

Fitness

Meal Plan

Daily Planner

M T W T F S S

Date _____

MUST DO TODAY:
- ☐ _____
- ☐ _____
- ☐ _____

SCHEDULE + TO-DOS

_____
_____
_____
_____
_____
_____
_____
_____
_____
_____
_____
_____
_____
_____
_____

APPOINTMENTS
_____
_____
_____
_____
_____

TODAY I'M GRATEFUL FOR:

NOTES:

Hydration

Fitness

Meal Plan

Daily Planner

M T W T F S S

Date _____

MUST DO TODAY:
- ☐
- ☐
- ☐

SCHEDULE + TO-DOS

APPOINTMENTS

TODAY I'M GRATEFUL FOR:

NOTES:

Hydration

Fitness

Meal Plan

Daily Planner

M T W T F S S

Date _____

MUST DO TODAY:
- ○
- ○
- ○

SCHEDULE + TO-DOS

APPOINTMENTS

TODAY I'M GRATEFUL FOR:

NOTES:

Hydration

Fitness

Meal Plan

Thank You!

We hope you enjoyed our Planner.

As a small family company, your feedback is verry important to us.

Please let us know how you like our book at:

adildaisy@gmail.com

CPSIA information can be obtained
at www.ICGtesting.com
Printed in the USA
BVHW062202190321
603091BV00016B/912